AI-Powered Business Success: 100 Prompts to Build, Scale, and Optimize Your Dream Venture

By Simon Foote ©Copyright 2024

Contents

Introduction 3
1. Market Research and Analysis 5
2. Business Plan Creation 8
3. Financial Planning and Forecasting 10
4. Branding and Identity Development 13
5. Marketing Strategy and Content Creation 15
6. Customer Persona and Target Audience Insights 17
7. Legal and Administrative Support 19
8. Sales Strategy and Proposal Writing 22
9. Product Development and Optimization 25
10. Operations and Process Optimization 27
Conclusion 30

Introduction

In the modern business world, agility, efficiency, and innovation are more critical than ever. The rise of artificial intelligence has ushered in a new era of possibilities, enabling entrepreneurs and professionals to automate processes, analyze data, and generate ideas at an unprecedented pace. But the real key to unlocking AI's transformative potential lies in how we guide it—through carefully crafted prompts.

This guide is your ultimate resource, offering **100 powerful AI prompts** designed to address every stage of the business lifecycle, from market research and financial planning to branding, operations, and sales strategy. Whether you're starting a new venture, scaling an existing business, or streamlining your processes, these prompts will empower you to harness AI effectively, saving time, cutting costs, and driving better results.

Dive in, and discover how AI can become your most valuable ally in building the business you've always envisioned. **It's time to work smarter, innovate faster, and stay ahead of the competition.** Let's get started!

1. Market Research and Analysis

1. **Prompt**: "Identify the top three competitors in the [industry/product] market and their strengths and weaknesses."
   Use: Helps refine competitive strategies and discover potential gaps in the market.
2. **Prompt**: "Analyze the growth trends of the [specific region/global] market for [product/service]."
   Use: Provides insights into future opportunities and market demands.
3. **Prompt**: "List five emerging technologies impacting the [industry] in the next 5 years."
   Use: Guides innovation efforts and resource planning for technological integration.
4. **Prompt**: "What are the top 3 challenges businesses face in the [specific market]?"

Use: Allows businesses to plan mitigation strategies for known industry challenges.

5. **Prompt**: "Provide a SWOT analysis for starting a [business type] in [region]."
   Use: Offers a holistic view of strengths, weaknesses, opportunities, and threats.

6. **Prompt**: "Summarize recent consumer behavior trends in [industry/product]."
   Use: Helps align marketing efforts with customer preferences.

7. **Prompt**: "Analyze the potential demand for [product/service] in [specific demographic]."
   Use: Validates target markets and estimates sales potential.

8. **Prompt**: "What are the average profit margins in the [industry]?"
   Use: Assists in setting pricing models and financial benchmarks.

9. **Prompt**: "List five untapped market opportunities for [product/service]."
   Use: Identifies niches for expansion and market differentiation.
10. **Prompt**: "What regulations impact businesses operating in the [specific industry]?"
    Use: Ensures compliance with industry-specific laws, avoiding penalties.

2. Business Plan Creation

1. **Prompt**: "Draft a business plan for a [business type] targeting [specific demographic]."
   Use: Provides a clear roadmap for startup operations and funding pitches.
2. **Prompt**: "Write a detailed mission and vision statement for [business]."
   Use: Establishes organizational values and long-term goals.
3. **Prompt**: "Outline the key elements of a scalable business model for [industry]."
   Use: Creates a sustainable structure for growth.
4. **Prompt**: "Create a detailed financial plan for the first year of [business type]."
   Use: Offers clarity on expected revenues, costs, and resource allocation.

5. **Prompt**: "Summarize the operational requirements for starting a [specific business]."
   Use: Lists essential steps, reducing startup inefficiencies.
6. **Prompt**: "List the top risks and mitigation strategies for a [business type]."
   Use: Prepares for potential challenges with actionable solutions.
7. **Prompt**: "What are the best distribution channels for [product/service]?"
   Use: Helps maximize reach and delivery efficiency.
8. **Prompt**: "Provide a step-by-step guide for setting up a [specific industry] business."
   Use: Breaks down complex tasks into manageable actions.
9. **Prompt**: "Create a staffing plan for the first year of a [specific business]."

Use: Ensures hiring aligns with operational priorities.

10. **Prompt**: "Design a growth strategy for a [business type] over five years."
    Use: Supports long-term scalability and resource optimization.

3. Financial Planning and Forecasting

1. **Prompt**: "Create a 12-month cash flow projection for a [business type]."
   Use: Maintains operational liquidity by tracking inflows and outflows.
2. **Prompt**: "Calculate the break-even point for [business type] with the following parameters: [inputs]."
   Use: Sets realistic sales and pricing goals to achieve profitability.
3. **Prompt**: "Generate best- and worst-case financial scenarios for [business]."

Use: Assists in preparing for varying economic outcomes.

4. **Prompt**: "What are common startup costs for a [specific business]?"
   Use: Avoids underestimating initial investments and identifies funding needs.

5. **Prompt**: "Outline the steps to secure funding for a [business type]."
   Use: Offers guidance for attracting investors or loans.

6. **Prompt**: "Develop an expense forecast for the first year of a [business type]."
   Use: Allocates resources strategically and avoids overspending.

7. **Prompt**: "What tax implications should [business type] owners consider?"
   Use: Ensures compliance with tax regulations while optimizing liabilities.

8. **Prompt**: "Provide a revenue projection for a [product/service] based on [parameters]."
   Use: Guides pricing and marketing strategies.
9. **Prompt**: "List 5 strategies for optimizing cash flow in a [specific business]."
   Use: Enhances financial stability by improving liquidity management.
10. **Prompt**: "Develop a financial risk management plan for [business type]."
    Use: Protects the business against unexpected losses.

4. Branding and Identity Development

1. **Prompt**: "Suggest a memorable brand name for [business type] targeting [specific audience]."
   Use: Creates a distinct identity that resonates with target customers.
2. **Prompt**: "Create a tagline for [business type] emphasizing [key benefit]."
   Use: Develops a concise, impactful slogan to highlight the brand's value.
3. **Prompt**: "List five logo design ideas for [business type]."
   Use: Guides graphic designers or DIY logo creation.
4. **Prompt**: "What colors and fonts best represent a [specific type of business]?"
   Use: Ensures visual branding aligns with industry and audience expectations.

5. **Prompt**: "Write a brand story for a [specific business]."
   Use: Builds an emotional connection with customers through storytelling.
6. **Prompt**: "What are three brand archetypes that fit [business type]?"
   Use: Defines the brand's personality to maintain consistency in messaging.
7. **Prompt**: "List ten potential domain names for [business name]."
   Use: Identifies online presence options for securing digital assets.
8. **Prompt**: "Create a tone of voice guide for [brand]."
   Use: Maintains uniformity in customer communication.
9. **Prompt**: "How can [business type] establish a strong online brand presence?"
   Use: Provides actionable steps for digital branding success.
10. **Prompt**: "Generate a unique value proposition for [business]."

Use: Articulates what sets the brand apart from competitors.

5. Marketing Strategy and Content Creation

1. **Prompt**: "Create a 30-day marketing campaign for [business type]."
   Use: Saves time while ensuring consistent outreach.
2. **Prompt**: "Suggest social media post ideas for [specific business/industry]."
   Use: Increases customer engagement with varied content.
3. **Prompt**: "What are the top five platforms for advertising [product/service]?"
   Use: Allocates advertising budget to the most effective channels.
4. **Prompt**: "Draft a newsletter for launching [business/product]."

Use: Drives awareness and excitement for new offerings.

5. **Prompt**: "What are the most effective digital marketing tactics for [industry]?"

   Use: Maximizes ROI from marketing investments.

6. **Prompt**: "Generate a content calendar for a [business type] targeting [audience]."

   Use: Ensures planned, strategic communication with customers.

7. **Prompt**: "Write a product launch press release for [product/service]."

   Use: Gains media attention and builds credibility.

8. **Prompt**: "Suggest email marketing strategies for engaging [specific audience]."

   Use: Nurtures leads and increases conversions.

9. **Prompt**: "Create a video script promoting [business/product]."

Use: Provides direction for compelling visual storytelling.
10. **Prompt**: "List 10 SEO-friendly blog topics for [business type]."
    Use: Boosts website traffic and enhances search rankings.

6. Customer Persona and Target Audience Insights

1. **Prompt**: "Create a persona for a typical [business type] customer, including goals and pain points."
   Use: Refines customer-focused strategies.
2. **Prompt**: "What are the buying triggers for [specific audience] in [industry]?"
   Use: Enhances marketing and sales approaches.
3. **Prompt**: "What communication styles resonate with [specific

demographic]?"

Use: Improves customer engagement through tailored messaging.

4. **Prompt**: "Describe the ideal customer journey for [business type]."

   Use: Optimizes interactions from lead generation to conversion.

5. **Prompt**: "What are the top objections customers might have about [product/service]?"

   Use: Prepares responses to overcome barriers to purchase.

6. **Prompt**: "List common behaviors of [target audience] when shopping online."

   Use: Aligns e-commerce strategies with customer habits.

7. **Prompt**: "What social media platforms do [specific audience] use most?"

   Use: Focuses social media marketing efforts effectively.

8. **Prompt**: "Create a psychographic profile for [business type] customers."
   Use: Adds depth to understanding customer motivations.
9. **Prompt**: "What are the primary concerns of [specific audience] in [industry]?"
   Use: Adjusts product/service to address pain points.
10. **Prompt**: "What motivates [specific demographic] to choose [product/service]?"
    Use: Informs messaging for higher conversions.

7. Legal and Administrative Support

1. **Prompt**: "What are the licensing requirements for [business type] in [region]?"
   Use: Ensures compliance with local regulations.

2. **Prompt**: "List the steps to register a [business type] in [specific country/region]."
   Use: Simplifies administrative processes.
3. **Prompt**: "What taxes apply to [business type] in [country/region]?"
   Use: Helps with financial compliance and planning.
4. **Prompt**: "Create a checklist for opening a [specific business] legally in [region]."
   Use: Organizes necessary actions for starting operations.
5. **Prompt**: "What are common legal pitfalls for [business type] owners?"
   Use: Reduces risks associated with legal oversights.
6. **Prompt**: "What insurance policies should a [business type] have?"
   Use: Protects against potential liabilities.

7. **Prompt**: "Draft a privacy policy for [business type]."
   Use: Ensures compliance with data protection laws.
8. **Prompt**: "What employment laws apply to [specific business/region]?"
   Use: Safeguards business operations from legal violations.
9. **Prompt**: "List the required permits for [business type] in [specific area]."
   Use: Avoids delays in operational approval.
10. **Prompt**: "How can a [business type] protect intellectual property?"
    Use: Secures unique business assets from theft or misuse.

8. Sales Strategy and Proposal Writing

1. **Prompt**: "Draft a sales proposal for [product/service] targeting [specific audience]."
   Use: Creates compelling pitches to secure clients.
2. **Prompt**: "What are the key elements of an effective pitch for [business type]?"
   Use: Enhances persuasiveness and client engagement.
3. **Prompt**: "Write a follow-up email for a potential client in [industry]."
   Use: Increases conversion rates by maintaining communication.
4. **Prompt**: "What are three strategies for upselling [product/service]?"
   Use: Boosts revenue from existing customers.
5. **Prompt**: "Create a sales call script for pitching [product/service]."

Use: Streamlines sales team interactions for consistency.

6. **Prompt**: "What are common objections to [product/service], and how to address them?"
   Use: Prepares sales teams to handle challenges effectively.

7. **Prompt**: "Generate an incentive plan for [business type] sales team."
   Use: Motivates employees to meet or exceed sales targets.

8. **Prompt**: "Write a product demo outline for [product/service]."
   Use: Ensures clear and impactful demonstrations.

9. **Prompt**: "What are the best networking practices for [business type]?"
   Use: Helps build valuable professional relationships.

10. **Prompt**: "How can [business type] create a strong referral program?"

Use: Leverages existing customers to acquire new leads.

9. Product Development and Optimization

1. **Prompt**: "Suggest innovative features for a [product/service] targeting [specific audience]."
   Use: Stays competitive and aligns with customer expectations.
2. **Prompt**: "How can [business type] improve [product/service] based on customer feedback?"
   Use: Enhances satisfaction and usability.
3. **Prompt**: "What are three cost-saving manufacturing methods for [product]?"
   Use: Reduces production expenses.
4. **Prompt**: "Draft a roadmap for developing [product/service]."
   Use: Organizes timelines and milestones.
5. **Prompt**: "What are five common issues in [product type], and how to resolve them?"

Use: Proactively improves quality control.

6. **Prompt**: "How can [business type] make [product/service] more eco-friendly?"

   Use: Meets sustainability goals and market demand.

7. **Prompt**: "What technologies can enhance [product/service] performance?"

   Use: Keeps offerings technologically relevant.

8. **Prompt**: "Draft a beta testing plan for [product]."

   Use: Gathers insights to refine products before launch.

9. **Prompt**: "What packaging options are most cost-effective for [product]?"

   Use: Balances cost savings with customer appeal.

10. **Prompt**: "Create a go-to-market strategy for [new product/service]."

Use: Ensures a successful product launch.

10. Operations and Process Optimization

1. **Prompt**: "Design an efficient workflow for [specific business process]."
   Use: Saves time and reduces bottlenecks in operations.
2. **Prompt**: "How can [business type] reduce operational costs by 20%?"
   Use: Improves profitability and sustainability.
3. **Prompt**: "What are the best tools for managing [business process]?"
   Use: Recommends software or methods for improved efficiency.
4. **Prompt**: "Create a staff scheduling plan for [business type]."
   Use: Ensures balanced workload distribution.

5. **Prompt**: "How can [business type] optimize inventory management?"
   Use: Reduces costs associated with overstock or shortages.
6. **Prompt**: "Suggest automation tools for [specific process]."
   Use: Streamlines repetitive tasks to save time.
7. **Prompt**: "What are the top performance metrics for [business type]?"
   Use: Tracks key indicators of success.
8. **Prompt**: "Draft a standard operating procedure for [task]."
   Use: Creates consistency and minimizes errors.
9. **Prompt**: "What strategies improve vendor relations for [business type]?"
   Use: Ensures smooth supply chain management.
10. **Prompt**: "What are the best practices for scaling [business type] operations?"

Use: Guides growth without overwhelming resources.

Conclusion

Establishing and growing a business in today's dynamic environment requires both strategic planning and efficient execution. Leveraging AI through thoughtful and tailored prompts provides an unparalleled advantage, offering solutions that save time, reduce costs, and amplify creativity. This comprehensive list of 100 AI prompts empowers entrepreneurs and business leaders to tackle critical areas such as market research, financial planning, branding, and operations with precision and ease.

From identifying market trends to optimizing workflows, these prompts are a testament to the versatility and transformative potential of AI in business. By using these tools, you not only enhance productivity but also unlock opportunities to innovate and stay competitive in an ever-evolving marketplace.

Remember, the key to maximizing the potential of AI lies in crafting specific, clear, and actionable prompts that align with your unique business goals. With this guide in hand, you are equipped to harness the power of AI as a strategic partner in your entrepreneurial journey. Let this be the start of a smarter, more efficient approach to building and managing your business.

Take action today and watch your vision come to life with the right AI tools and strategies!

www.ingramcontent.com/pod-product-compliance
Lightning Source LLC
Chambersburg PA
CBHW070959220526
45471CB00007B/3094